101
Soul
Seeds

for
Reinventing
Yourself

D1203522

Copyright © Anamchara Books, 2021.

All rights reserved. This book or any portion thereof may
not be reproduced or used in any manner whatsoever
without the express written permission of the publisher
except for the use of brief quotations in a book review.

Anamchara Books
Vestal, New York 13850
www.AnamcharaBooks.com

Paperback ISBN: 978-1-62524-839-8 (*IngramSpark edition*)
eBook ISBN: 978-1-62524-822-0

Cover design and interior layout by Micaela Grace.
Plant drawings by Microvone (Dreamstime.com).

101
Soul Seeds

for Reinventing
Yourself

KAREN SALITA

Introduction

When we were children, adults loved to ask us what we wanted to be when we grew up. We changed our minds often. No idea was too fanciful; nothing was off-limits. As we grew up, the world around us began to guide our options, rewarding our socially acceptable choices and frowning upon desires that deviated from the norm. Our actions and decisions led us in particular directions—some of which worked for us and some of which did not.

Over time, many of us discover that we want to move in new directions and show up in the world in new ways. We decide to reinvent ourselves. But this is easier said than done. There are many voices in our heads telling us that what we desire is selfish, unrealistic, or downright scary. But there are also voices in our heads telling us that we're talented, capable, and courageous. So which voices should we listen to? And how do we tune in to the inner guidance system that broadcasts messages that will truly benefit us?

101 Soul Seeds for Reinventing Yourself is a guidebook to empower your heart and soul on this transformational journey. Along the way you'll learn to gather and embrace all the parts of yourself that you discounted, hid away, or left behind. Through a process of creative exploration, you'll shift from feeling fractured to feeling whole as you begin to integrate these pieces back into the fullness of your experience. It's my hope that this book will help you reinvent your relationship with all the unique facets of yourself, allowing you to redesign your life in ways that are both meaningful and liberating.

The first paragraph of each Soul Seed introduces an impactful idea that will support your current process or encourage you to think in new, empowering ways. The second paragraph is a meditation of sorts through which you can explore these concepts from the perspective of your own voice. If you find them to be encouraging, you can return to them again and again as a reminder of what's possible for you. The third part of each Soul Seed is a quote that drives the core concept home.

Whether you're hearing and considering these ideas for the first time or the hundredth time, I truly hope they energize you for your journey ahead.

— Karen Salita

1.

Reinventing yourself is less about transforming yourself and more about transforming how you're showing up in the world. You are already you, but are you showing up as the fullest, most complete version of yourself? When you dig down to the roots of who you are, you'll discover the answers you seek already exist at the seed level, your Soul-Seed level. As you identify the seeds that feel most meaningful, you can nourish them—and you'll begin to flower!

I am the gardener of my life. I take responsibility for the care and feeding of my well-being. I may have buried the seeds of myself long ago and left them unattended and unnourished, but I am now ready to give them my attention and my love, and to allow those aspects of myself to flourish.

Do you have the courage
to bring forth this work?
The treasures that are hidden inside you
are hoping you will say yes.

—JACK GILBERT

2.

Beware the dreaded land of "almost." In this space, your job, your health, and your life are *almost* good enough and you're *almost* happy. "Almost" has the appearance of being desirable on the outside (you've worked so hard for it!), but on the inside it leaves you with a persistent nagging, aching, itchy feeling that says, "This isn't quite right!" "Almost" is no place to live. So pack your bags—it's time to leave the city limits and see what lies outside your comfort zone. Once you do, you'll wonder why you stayed in "almost" for so long.

I trust that my discomfort is my spirit giving me a message. It wants me to pay attention because my action is needed to make a change. This is not where I'm meant to be, so it's time to explore a new way of being for myself.

Pearls don't lie on the seashore.
If you want one, you must dive for it.

—CHINESE PROVERB

3.

Those of us who grew up in the 1980s are likely familiar with Choose-Your-Own-Adventure books. If we didn't like the ending of the book, we could go back and make different choices in each chapter, leading to different stories and outcomes for the main character. Our lives are also a Choose-Your-Own-Adventure story. Just because we find ourselves in a particular environment or a specific situation doesn't mean it's the end of the story. While we may not be able to go back and change our past, we have the ability to change our stories moving forward.

My life is fluid, dynamic, and always evolving. Though some of the choices I'm faced with are difficult, I recognize I do indeed have the power to choose. And every choice I make has the ability to bring me closer to the life I envision for myself.

You are only one decision away
from a totally different life.

—ZIG ZIGLAR

4.

Every year, car manufacturers reinvent their most popular models and release them with new-and-improved features. We should be no different. Life is full of opportunities to upgrade our experiences and our options. Allowing ourselves to remain unchanged is like bypassing the opportunity for GPS and traction control. Yes, it requires some extra research and development, but it is so worth it!

I'm proud of the person I am, but I'm not done becoming the person I'm meant to be. I seek opportunities to be inspired by others who are living the quality of life I desire, so I may have examples for my own life's design.

There are two ways you can live:
you can devote your life to staying in your comfort zone
or you can work on your freedom.

—MICHAEL A. SINGER

5.

We were born to be creative. From our earliest moments, we've been creating. As children, we may have made our own songs, stories, forts, or games. As teenagers and young adults, we were likely creating thoughts, ideas, and idealistic plots. Our creative nature is inherent within us. Along with creating, we're masters of re-creating—taking what already exists within our lives and reimagining, reshaping, and rebuilding it to match the inspired vision we hold. We're never finished creating our life; we simply continue to redesign the nature of our creation.

I find deep inspiration in my abilities to redesign my life for the better. I'm fully aware that with creativity comes uncertainty, and from uncertainty comes a world of possibility. I call upon my own courage to face the unknown with a curious spirit, an inspired heart, and a creative mind.

What is creativity?
The relationship between a human being
and the mysteries of inspiration.

—ELIZABETH GILBERT

6.

When parents send their children off to the first day of school each year, they often take photographs to document how much the kids grow and change over the years. We adults should also acknowledge and celebrate how much we continue to grow and change. We're much wiser today than we were five years ago, and five years from now we'll marvel at how much more we've experienced and accomplished. Whatever our age, we have the wonderful ability to shift our attention and intention to reinvent ourselves again and again.

When I think of the best age to embark on a new endeavor or adventure, the answer is . . . now! Always now—or very soon—at any age. The possibilities for my life are endless, and it's never too late for me to learn or explore something new.

> Human beings are works in progress
> that mistakenly think they're finished.
>
> —DANIEL GILBERT

7.

It's natural to feel hesitant when we embark on a personal journey without a perfected plan and a detailed map. But if we wait for a perfect plan, there's a good chance we'll never leave our driveway. Sometimes we just have to hit the road and head in the right direction. Often, the path that gets us where we want to go wasn't even on the map in the first place.

I am an explorer of my dreams and desires.
The path ahead of me is not always clear and
that's half the fun. Each bend in the road
reveals new discoveries and choices. I trust
I have the knowledge and tools to navigate
this uncertain landscape, and what I don't
already know I will learn along the way.

A journey of a thousand miles
begins with a single step.

—LAO TZU

8.

When we're not sure which direction to travel on our transformative journeys, we might benefit from a good *scavenger hunt*. Similar to the childhood game, this activity involves collecting ideas that capture our interest and attention from the world around us. Magazines, media, podcasts, books, YouTube videos, crafts, clubs, and conferences can all reveal a treasure trove of topics to indicate where we most enjoy spending our time and energy. When looking to develop ourselves in new ways, collecting themes that spark our interest can set us in motion in the right direction.

When I'm feeling lost, I need only to direct my attention to those subjects in which I lose myself. When time is also lost because it passed without notice, I know I have actually found myself within the ideas that have consumed my attention. When I invest my energy in these ideas, I truly begin to know myself.

> Tell me to what you pay attention
> and I will tell you who you are.

—JOSÉ ORTEGA Y GASSET

9.

Children love playing dress-up to experiment with how different identities look and feel. As adults, we can also try on identities to see how they look and feel. How would the person we'd like to be dress and act? How would they spend their time? With whom would they spend their time? Experimenting with new ways of being allows us to feel what it might be like to reinvent ourselves in these ways. Just because we're no longer children doesn't mean we can't try on different versions of ourselves for size.

When I imagine the person I'd like to become, I can also imagine the choices I'd make each day. When I align my choices with that new individual's, I get to experience life from another perspective. When living life in this way feels inspiring, then I know I'm on the right path.

> Never mind searching for who you are.
> Search for the person you aspire to be.

—ROBERT BRAULT

10.

When other people make judgements about our journey, their judgements are more about their own personal insecurities and doubts than they are about us. These judgements can land like insects on our windshield: if we focus on them while we're driving, they'll become all we see, and we'll lose sight of the road. Learning to ignore the "bugs" allows us to see our journey ahead more clearly. The judgements may still be there, but they'll no longer distract our vision.

I'm aware that other people may not support my choices and dreams, and that's okay. Their opinions are part of their own journey, not mine. I choose to remain focused on the path that feels right for me, and if I deviate from my path or change my course, it's because I have chosen to do so. Nobody else will choose for me.

What other people think of me
is none of my business.

—AL-ANON PRINCIPLE

11.

Having a *buddy system* may be one of the biggest guarantees of future success when it comes to taking on challenging goals. Spending time with like-minded people who support our journeys, as well as our evolving identities, has been proven to increase confidence, self-esteem, and resilience in the face of adversity. A "buddy" can be a friend, a mentor, or a hired coach who prioritizes our success and holds us accountable for the goals we set for ourselves. Sometimes, just knowing someone's cheering us on is all we need to keep moving forward. And being that buddy for someone else increases our confidence and follow-through, too.

Because I'm human and I'm partly driven by a desire to look good, as well as a desire to avoid looking bad, having an accountability partner helps me follow through with my commitments. And knowing that person believes in me means I can borrow certainty when mine feels challenged.

If you want to fast, go alone.
If you want to go far, go together.

—AFRICAN PROVERB

12.

We all have a virtual radio station playing in our minds. We tend to alternate between the station playing positive, self-affirming programming filled with messages of encouragement and the station playing disparaging, fearful content designed to discourage us. We often accept the station that's playing as if we have no control over the dial. But we do have control! We can mentally change the channel when negative messages are dominating our airwaves by choosing to switch to more supportive, affirming mental messages.

I recognize that my thoughts are often just nervous energy seeking an outlet. And quite often the chatter in my mind isn't even my own—it's the voice of my mother or my childhood teacher or an ex-lover trying to convince me of something that isn't true. I don't need to listen to this unproductive noise. Instead, I will change the channel.

Where the mind goes, energy flows.

—YOGA PRINCIPLE

13.

Sometimes we're launched into emergency management mode because something in our lives has fallen apart. Though it may feel like a great catastrophe, disruption can be good as it forces us to get creative with finding alternative ways to navigate life. Just as inconvenient road construction can force us off the highway and onto interesting side streets, disruption in life can encourage us to get out of routines and relationships that aren't serving us. It may be incredibly uncomfortable in the moment, but disruption can help us find new ways of being that work better for our lives.

I welcome opportunities to stretch, grow, and think outside the box, and I understand that these opportunities may be brilliantly disguised as impossible situations. I will look at this challenge through the eyes of my future self, who understands the unexpected advantages of being forced to find a creative solution for a messy situation.

Sometimes good things fall apart
so better things can fall together.

—(ATTRIBUTED TO) MARILYN MONROE

14.

If difficult or painful experiences are the catalyst for our reinvention process, *grief can become our gift*. Grief has the power to encourage us to make positive changes in our own life or to have a positive impact on someone else's. The old adage "necessity is the mother of invention" highlights the idea that a great need—or a great loss—often drives positive change. Going through hardship forces us to adapt, developing our resilience and a sense of empowerment along the way. If we can learn to see our present hardship for the gift it will be in the future, we can gain comfort and strength for the journey ahead.

When circumstances eject me from my comfort zone, I can become a time traveler and leap into my future self. From there, I can see the value of the past, which empowers me in the present. My grief becomes my gift when it's my catalyst for change, helping me to reach a better future.

> Not till we are lost . . .
> do we begin to find ourselves.

—HENRY DAVID THOREAU

15.

Changing the course of your life means leaving the past behind you. However, just like while driving a car, if you set your sights on a new destination but keep your eyes only on the rear-view mirror, you'll have a very hard time getting to the place you'd like to be. You have to focus on the road ahead. It's time to let go of where you were and the person you've been, so you can explore new horizons and new ways of being.

My life is a journey and I'm in the driver's seat. I choose to move forward without needing to look back. I'm grateful for all the experiences I've had and the things I've seen, but I have a full tank of gas and somewhere I'd like to be. Time to get this show on the road!

Don't look back!
You're not going that way.

—ANONYMOUS

16.

Embrace feeling stuck! Stuck is where the magic happens. They say *necessity is the mother of invention.* I say necessity is the mother of reinvention! When things are going fine—not bad, not good—it's easy to stay the course without making meaningful and impactful changes. When something is noticeably missing or not working and we feel stuck . . . good! That means we're now uncomfortable enough to start brainstorming possible positive changes we can make.

I may be in an uncomfortable place, but I know in my heart this is the catalyst for positive change. I give myself permission, without judgement, to unleash my creativity and brainstorm every silly, crazy, off-the-wall solution I can think of to this challenge I'm facing. Within the space of my own creativity lie many wonderful solutions I haven't thought of yet.

The true sign of intelligence is not knowledge but imagination.

—(ATTRIBUTED TO) ALBERT EINSTEIN

17.

What we put in our bodies has a tremendous impact on our thoughts, our emotions, and our productivity, so paying attention to our *care and feeding* is of utmost importance during the transformative process. While the brain comprises just 2 percent of our total body weight, it uses up to 20 percent of our energy resources. Instead of consuming low-quality, low-octane fuel, we can ditch the sugar and processed foods and opt for a colorful, varied diet rich in whole, plant-based foods and brain-nurturing nutrients like Omega-3 fatty acids. This will ensure that our brain's tank is full of quality nourishment for the journey.

Dear Body, I know I haven't always been particularly kind to you, and I admit I've taken for granted your miraculous nature. But I'm ready to give you the attention you deserve. I understand that my brain needs nourishment so it can help me thrive. From this day forward, I will be mindful about what I feed us. I may not always be perfect, but I promise to always try.

To keep the body in good health is a duty,
for otherwise we shall not be able to . . .
keep our mind strong and clear.

—GAUTAMA BUDDHA

18.

Change is inevitable, not just around us, but also within us. We change ourselves to adapt to an ever-changing world, but most of the time we do it unconsciously and unintentionally. Often, we allow the dynamic environment around us to influence our thoughts, emotions, and behaviors—we become the *effect* of our environment, which leaves us feeling powerless. By choosing to become intentional with our personal reinvention, we take ownership of the process and we make the unconscious conscious. We empower ourselves by becoming the *cause*, rather than the effect, of our lives.

Oh wondrous world, filled with so many opportunities, and so many challenges, please help me to notice those moments when I feel powerless in my response to my ever-changing environment. Help me to pause and ask, "Is it really true? Am I really powerless? What do I want to feel in this moment? And is there an action I can take that is consistent with how I want to feel?" Please help me to be the cause and not the effect in my life.

Until you make the unconscious conscious, it will direct your life and you will call it fate.

—CARL JUNG

19.

Physical pain is often the body's way of protecting us by asking that we slow down and make a change in our activities. Similarly, emotional pain can be a loving message from our inner being asking also that we slow down and reassess a situation. It may encourage us to ask, "Are my activities healthy and productive? Are the people I'm involved with helping me to grow into the best version of myself? Is my job moving me closer to or further away from my goals?" Pain can be a catalyst for positive change, and while it may not feel good in the moment, it often contains gifts that can be appreciated only in hindsight.

I have the courage to sit with my pain and ask it what important messages it holds for me. What in my life is not working for me right now? What kinds of choices are available to me that would change these situations for the better? How might I look back on this pain one, two, or five years from now? Could I then see it as a gift?

Your pain is the breaking of the shell that encloses your understanding.

—KAHLIL GIBRAN

20.

If you feel guilty about focusing on your own wholeness and well-being rather than the well-being of others, please remember this: You cannot give fully to those you love if you are not fulfilled yourself. You cannot fill other people's cups if your own pitcher is empty. When you focus on finding that which fulfills you, your well-being spills over to benefit those around you. The very act of seeking wholeness is an expression of generosity, both toward yourself and toward those you love.

I am capable of loving others only when I love myself first. I love myself most when I feel connected to my passions, my goals, my potential, and my spirit.

We need to love ourselves if we want
our kids to love themselves.
We don't necessarily have to love them more;
we have to love ourselves more.

—GLENNON DOYLE

21.

Resistance is what we experience when it feels like something in our world is working against us. We start to view life as difficult, uncomfortable, and negative. But what if the resistance is actually there to serve us and to make us stronger? In the fitness world, it's called *resistance training*. Lifting weights that are just beyond our ability helps us develop the capability to lift those weights. Experiencing resistance in life helps us to build the resilience, strength, patience, and bravery needed to navigate daily life and thrive.

So if you want to develop your resilience muscles, look for more resistance!

I grow stronger every day with each situation that challenges me. Just as I look upon my younger self with great compassion for all that I had not yet learned, I can look upon myself now through the eyes of my older, wiser self, also with great compassion for all that I will accomplish.

The resistance that you fight
physically in the gym
and the resistance that you fight in life
can only build a strong character.

—ARNOLD SCHWARZENEGGER

22.

Many of us are recovering perfectionists. And while we know in our heads that things don't have to be perfect, we often find that our hearts haven't gotten the message. We may be flying high and feeling triumphant when all our plans and actions are falling into place, but the moment our efforts return sub-par results, we crash.

It's important to look at all your experiences for what they are—opportunities to learn and grow. Don't let unexpected outcomes stop your momentum. Use them as stepping stones to keep moving forward.

I understand that perfection is just an illusion, and I embrace the opportunity to grow beyond my limits. I'm grateful for all the times things haven't gone as planned and I learned to be more skillful because of it. I look forward to practicing my resilience by embracing imperfection.

Worry pretends to be necessary
but serves no useful purpose.

—ECKHART TOLLE

23.

Sometimes we feel the need to shrink our desires so we don't draw too much attention to ourselves. Keeping our desires small because we're afraid of being judged by others is a lot like keeping a large plant confined in a small container so it doesn't continue to grow. When we conceal our dreams and desires, we deny our very nature, which is to emerge, expand, and flourish. As the gardeners of our lives, the greatest gift we can give ourselves is permission to grow.

I am a seed of possibility planted, and it is my destiny to grow. I will honor this opportunity by nourishing myself with positive thoughts and influences, and I will surround myself with like-minded souls who are eager to grow with me. As I allow my potential to unfold, I find the sense of wholeness I have been seeking.

And the day came
when the risk to remain tight as a bud
was more painful than
the risk it took to blossom.

—ELIZABETH APPELL

24.

O ur ultimate desire on the reinvention jour- ney is to connect with our *True Self.* As a deep, intuitive wisdom residing within our core, our True Self knows and understands what we want and need for our lives to feel complete. This elemental part of ourselves was our *primary self* when we were children, before the world began imposing its beliefs and assumptions on us. The True Self feels worthy and isn't concerned with the opinions and expectations of others. When we are able to focus on creating a life that satisfies us, rather than prioritizing the satisfaction of others, we are connecting with our True Self.

When I get lost in conversation with another person, I'm showing up as my True Self. When time passes without notice because I'm deeply interested and engaged in an activity, I'm engaged as my True Self. When I experience self-assurance and certainty with a sense of calm, I'm experiencing my True Self. My True Self is who I am when the rest of the world disappears.

Never get tired of being your true original self. You are too special to be anything other than a reflection of your true identity.

—EDMOND MBIAKA

25.

Your True Self is a puzzle gifted to you by your Source. Much like a parent, your Source knows that gifting you a fully formed and completed puzzle won't bring you as much lasting joy and satisfaction as tasking you with the challenge and gratification of working diligently on your puzzle over the course of your life. Feeling incomplete on the journey toward your True Self is simply a sign that your puzzle is in process and that you have a desire to put the pieces together in a meaningful way.

I take comfort in knowing that this journey toward my True Self is part of a greater plan for me. Not only is there nothing wrong with feeling incomplete at this point in my life, I'm aware that everything about this puzzle is aligned for my greatest good. I will embrace my journey as the gift that it is, and I will find joy in the process as well.

The solution often turns out more beautiful than the puzzle.

—RICHARD DAWKINS

26.

Trying new things often gives our comfort zone a good workout. As children we were experts at trying new things because everything was new and exciting. As adults, we've become comfortable with routine and our "new things" muscles have weakened. Giving ourselves a regular workout of trying new things not only strengthens our ability to overcome the anxiety of the unknown, it also allows us to encounter ideas and activities we never knew existed. The thing that could change our lives might be something we haven't experienced yet.

When I try new things that challenge me, I get better at managing my own discomfort and insecurities. The more I practice stepping out of my comfort zone, the stronger and more skilled I become. The more experiences I have, the more I learn about myself and the things that set my soul on fire.

Life begins at the end of your comfort zone.

—NEALE DONALD WALSCH

27.

In the video game world, players can acquire special performance boosts through *power-ups*. In the real world, we can power-up our reinvention process through exercise! Getting the heart pumping through physical activity several times a week has been scientifically proven to change the physiology and function of the hippocampus region of the brain. This results in increased focus and attention, improved long-term memory, and elevated mood. Finding ways to make exercise fun and practicing it consistently delivers both immediate and long-term benefits, not only for our physical bodies, but for our mental and emotional well-being, too.

When I move my body, I'm reminded of the absolute miracle that I am. I'm in awe of everything that must work perfectly on a cellular level for me to move and function. My mind, body, and spirit are working together so that I may thrive. I will honor this miracle by giving my body the attention it deserves, and in turn my body will honor me, allowing me to become physically and mentally stronger.

Movement is a medicine for creating change
in a person's physical, emotional,
and mental states

—CAROL WELCH-BARIL

28.

One thing's for sure—change is risky. There are no guarantees that it will turn out exactly the way we envision. But another thing is also true: It could turn out better. The most important factor in this equation is not strength, or skill, or status—it is courage. It's standing in the face of the unpredictable and the unknown and declaring that we aren't going to settle for a life that doesn't inspire us. It's about mustering up all the courage we have and taking a chance.

You will never know what's possible if you don't try.

Courage is a muscle I can build. The more I practice it with small challenges in my life, the more I'll be prepared to use it with the bigger ones.

Life shrinks or expands
in proportion to one's courage.

—GORDON LIVINGSTON

29.

When tragedy strikes and life as we know it changes in an instant, it's easy to feel victimized. It's okay to feel sad in the moments when we're mourning what we've lost, but choosing to stay in this powerless place is a tremendous disservice to ourselves. We're meant to lead remarkable lives—even if there's pain involved and life doesn't look the way we expected. Courage and vulnerability become our superpowers when we make the choice to stand up in the face of adversity. We can choose to follow in the footsteps of those who have experienced tremendous hardship and gone on to lead extraordinary lives.

I'm sitting at a crossroads, with my life as I've known it behind me. In front of me lie two paths: one leads to grief, suffering, and powerlessness; the other leads to hope, compassion, and empowerment. I find comfort in knowing that I'm not alone—many others have walked down this same path. I also know that in every moment I can choose how I respond to my situation. Today I choose to focus on the good and the things I can change. Today I choose the path of hope.

The impediment to action becomes the action. What stands in the way becomes the way.

—MARCUS AURELIUS

30.

Sometimes we find ourselves at rock bottom—that harsh wake-up call where the momentum of our own gravity collides so hard with reality that it knocks us silly. It's important to understand that our pain has a purpose. Rock bottom is like a hideous alarm clock that wakes us up from our previous narrative and asks us if we want to change the story. But there's beauty, too, in the rock bottom—the ground is finally beneath our feet and we now know which way is up.

In these moments of suffering, I pray for strength, clarity, and wisdom so that I may see my journey from the perspective of the Divine. I know that I embody the love of my Source, who sees my potential, even when I do not. My pain has a purpose: it will help me grow and be an inspiration for others who struggle like I did.

Rock bottom became the solid foundation on which I rebuilt my life.

—J. K. ROWLING

31.

We all hold deep desires for certain outcomes in our lives and feeling a sense of *hope* for these outcomes helps fuel our journey. For most people, hope is the yearning that tomorrow will be better than today. But this definition of hope can rely on luck and forces outside ourselves, not encouraging us or building our confidence in the likelihood of a better tomorrow. Instead, we can choose to envision hope as the belief that our *efforts* will create more positive future outcomes. This empowers and strengthens our optimism.

The more I experience and the more I experiment, the more I grow my abilities. The more I grow my abilities, the more empowered I am to make choices that will positively impact my outcomes. When I feel empowered, I feel a tremendous sense of hope and optimism that I can guide my life in the direction of my desires.

Hope is a verb with its sleeves rolled up.

—DAVID ORR

32.

It's easy to get stuck spinning our wheels in the muck of things we actually have no control over. When we start expending time and energy on people and circumstances we can't change, we end up exhausted and depleted without making any headway. Instead, when we identify those aspects of our situation that we can directly impact, we become empowered to take action in meaningful ways. By focusing on *controlling the controllables*, we're able to direct our attention and efforts toward activities that can help us make real progress toward our goals.

I understand that I have a choice in how I respond to events and circumstances. When I look at the intersection between things that matter and things I can control, I find the space for focusing my efforts. And even when things seem beyond my control, I can still impact my effort and my attitude.

When we are no longer
able to change a situation,
we are challenged to change ourselves.

—VIKTOR FRANKL

33.

If you've ever sailed on a sailboat, then you know it's very rare to follow a straight course to your destination. Sailors are constantly adjusting their sails to respond to the changing wind. The resulting path is full of zigs and zags and course corrections. Life is no different. Though you may have your sights set on a particular point on the horizon, you can be certain the wind will change often, and so will your course. But this is what makes the journey interesting, exciting, and fun!

The more I practice changing direction in my life, the better I become at navigating my ever-changing environment. The more skilled I become, the more confident I feel, and the more likely I am to reach my destination.

The pessimist complains about the wind;
the optimist expects it to change;
the realist adjusts the sails.

—WILLIAM ARTHUR WARD

34.

Beware the *big changes trap*. When we're setting out on the personal reinvention journey, it's easy to fall into the trap of setting the bar too high. We become disempowered when we give ourselves an ultimatum with larger-than-life goals. We are then like athletes who begin training by competing at a national level high-jump competition. When we don't do well on our first attempt, we feel the sting of failure and are less likely to try again. Instead, start training with low-bar goals that you know you can clear; then gradually raise them over time while developing strength, skills, and confidence.

I have big dreams and goals, and I'm excited to begin making the small changes that will help me achieve them. Every milestone I hit will help to remind me why I chose this journey and will give me a chance to celebrate my progress along the way.

Even the most complex and
creative of human abilities
can be broken down into its component skills,
each of which can be
practiced, practiced, practiced.

—ANGELA DUCKWORTH

35.

Often, we interpret failure as a catastrophic indication that we are less valuable or worthy. But when we look closely, failing is nothing more than achieving results that are different from those we hoped for and expected. Studies have shown that we can benefit and grow from these unexpected detours by reframing and rerouting the experience. If taking a left leads to a dead end, we can go back and try taking a right. If an outcome is disappointing, we can consider all the things we've learned from the experience and how those lessons will benefit us in the future.

I believe I can cultivate success through my efforts and actions, and I understand it may not happen on the first, second, or even the third try. If my outcomes aren't what I expect, I'll consider it feedback, not failure. Then I'll apply what I've learned toward developing a new strategy for myself moving forward.

Failure is not the opposite of success,
it's part of success.

—ARIANNA HUFFINGTON

36.

When toddlers are learning to walk, we don't view their unsuccessful attempts as "failing"; we simply see it as "falling." Like any young enthusiast trying something new, we too are bound to fall before we take our first successful steps. Each time we fall, we learn something new about our process, and we gain important skills for our next attempt. *Falling* happens when we stumble and pull ourselves up to try again. Failing happens only when we stumble and choose to give up.

When I imagine myself as an athlete or a dancer, I'm reminded of the importance of learning to be masterful at falling. In this space, losing my balance, colliding with an obstacle, and even crashing are all part of the game. The more I allow myself to have experiences where things don't go as planned, the more skillful I become at getting back on track.

I have not failed.
I've just found 10,000 ways that don't work.

—THOMAS EDISON

37.

When our personal transformation journey is motivated by self-criticism, our ability to create positive change is dramatically diminished. It's like wearing dissatisfaction glasses, which cause us to view everything that happens through the lens of "I'm not good enough." However, when we cultivate compassion for ourselves and our experiences, we trade self-criticism for self-appreciation. Choosing to say, "I may not be perfect, but I'm still pretty amazing, and I'm working hard for positive change," empowers us and prepares us for the bumps ahead.

I see the good in myself and I choose to celebrate it. I feel compassion for myself and my desires for growth and change. I know that I am enough, exactly as I am, and I'm also excited to grow into the person I'm becoming.

When you are compassionate with yourself, you trust in your soul, which you let guide your life. Your soul knows the geography of your destiny better than you do.

—JOHN O'DONOHUE

38.

When we're pursuing big desires in life, it's easy to start taking ourselves too seriously. When we become rigid about our experiences and our expectations, it's like placing a tourniquet on our journey that cuts off the blood flow to our desires and dreams. Big desires need flexibility and circulation to grow and expand. The best way to do this is by lightening up and having fun with the process.

My desire is to experience the joy of feeling alive. I want this, not only as an outcome, but as a characteristic of my journey as well. I acknowledge that I don't need to take myself so seriously, and by lightening up a little I can move closer to my goals and still have a really good time.

> Life isn't as serious as
> the mind makes it out to be.
>
> —ECKHART TOLLE

39.

I highly recommend not *shoulding* on yourself. It can be messy and unpleasant. *Shoulding* happens when you fill your head with all the ideas about who you *should* be and what your life *should* look like. When you *should* on yourself, you create a narrow view of life based on judgements about what's "worthy" or "good" or "sensible." *Shoulds* neglect what you truly want, they embody somebody else's ideals, and they restrict your options for success and happiness. Instead, when you embrace your *imagination* for what you really want, an expansive landscape of possibility opens up. More pleasant, indeed!

Now I lay me down to sleep, I pray that no more shoulds I'll keep. I'll free my mind for flow and play, and creative ways to spend my day. I'll count ideas like counting sheep, and pile ideas until knee deep. And when my ideas overflow, the best will shimmer and then I'll know. Out of the darkness and into the light, my life and my future will shine so bright.

It is a natural process to become your own person, to find your voice, convictions, and opinions, and to challenge and shed the Shoulds that no longer serve your evolving beliefs.

—ELLE LUNA

40.

When you feel you're getting bogged down in the heavy details of your journey, imagine yourself in a helicopter, moving higher and higher above the Earth. As you watch the ground beneath you fall away, you notice the details of things that seemed so big are suddenly very small. You can now see the vast landscape and it gives perspective to those small details. Allow yourself to see the big picture and realize that the big details aren't so big after all.

I give thanks for my ability to see the big picture of my life and the people in it. From way up here, things feel peaceful, and I'm empowered to navigate my landscape with ease. I can see that the details aren't quite as complicated as they may seem on the ground. I look forward to visiting my big picture any time I'd like to gain some perspective on my situation.

Life is about perspective
and how you look at something . . .
ultimately, you have to zoom out.

—WHITNEY WOLFE HERD

41.

Somehow, many of us got the memo that we're not supposed to pursue something in life unless we're good at it. That's a terrible memo! Here's a much better memo: We should pursue things in life *because* we're not good at them. That's how we get good at them. In fact, we should embrace being terrible at our new pursuits for a while. Then we can celebrate every improvement along the way. Pretty soon, people will be commenting about how good we are at the things we're doing, and saying how they wish they could do them too.

When I close my eyes, I can see myself as a child, eager and excited for the many new experiences that were available to me. A new instrument, a new language, a new sport . . . I was terrible at them all in the beginning, but not for long. I can choose new experiences today, too. I may be terrible in the beginning, but I won't be for long.

The willingness to show up changes us.
It makes us a little braver each time.

—BRENÉ BROWN

42.

Children's eyes see the world as something new to be explored. Their minds aren't yet cluttered with interpretations and expectations. To them, anything is possible. In Zen Buddhism, they call this state of mind *shoshin*, or "beginner's mind." But shoshin isn't reserved only for children. Rather than disregarding new information because we think we know better, approaching our world with the curiosity, receptivity, and wonder of *beginner's mind* allows us to see and capture opportunities we might otherwise miss.

I approach the world around me like a curious child, eager to learn and grow. I welcome new information and new experiences that will help me to see life in novel and creative ways. My mind is open, and I'm eager for new possibilities.

In the beginner's mind
there are many possibilities,
but in the expert's mind there are few.

—SHUNRYU SUZUKI

43.

A key component of the personal reinvention process is learning to develop our *student mentality*. When we choose to see ourselves as "works in progress," we can appreciate the fact that we're learning as we go. We can take notes and reflect on what does and doesn't work for us. Then we can shift our strategies to better address the issues at hand. Embracing our student mentality allows us to see obstacles not as barriers to our success but as challenges that hold valuable lessons.

I am an apprentice of my life. Every day I'm making new observations, learning new skills, and applying new techniques for mastering the art of living. My teacher is called Experience, and I receive wonderful feedback when I make mistakes, which happens often. Every mistake helps me improve, and my confidence is growing along the way. I'm proud of my accomplishments, and I can't wait to see what I learn next.

Curiosity is the wick in the candle of learning.

—WILLIAM ARTHUR WARD

44.

Being a good student of the reinvention process means mastering a simple equation:

Desire + Potential + Consistent Action =
Positive Change.

Your *desire* is your intention for change; it's less about wanting to achieve something, and more about being the kind of person who achieves that thing. Aligning with the *potential* of your desires means understanding the small, actionable steps you can take to move forward. Then, making consistent, daily choices and taking *consistent action* over time will help you narrow the gap between where you are and where you want to be.

My desires are more about *being* than they are about doing or getting. But I also know that when I *do* the steps necessary to move forward, I *get* to experience life in a way that is filled with meaning for me. I don't have to overthink the process, I just have to be clear about what I want and begin taking the necessary steps to get there.

In order to do the things
which are impossible for you,
you need to change yourself, and better still,
transform yourself into something new!

—MEHMET MURAT ILDAN

45.

Sometimes we wake up and realize that our lives have become wrapped up in identities that don't allow our true selves to be fully expressed. We might find ourselves here through parenthood, career, or a dysfunctional relationship. If the identity we chose fulfilled our immediate needs at the time but now leaves parts of ourselves neglected and undeveloped, we may end up feeling resentful. When this happens, it's important to give attention to those discarded or unattended parts of ourselves. Choosing to incorporate our fragmented or concealed parts back into the whole of our experience allows us to show up in more fulfilling ways.

Who I am and who I've been are important to me. But there are other parts of myself that require my attention now. I have neglected many interests and desires in life because they weren't priorities in the past. It's okay for me to focus on these now. I deserve the experience of the fullness of myself, and I'm now choosing to make this a priority.

One of the greatest tragedies in life
is to lose your own sense of self
and accept the version of you that is expected by
everyone else.

—K. L. TOTH

46.

When friends and family ask us why we're choosing to go in a new direction, we may not yet have the words to describe our thoughts, feelings, and motivations for change. Quite often, the only voice that can express our deep, heart-felt desire for personal transformation is our *inner voice*, and it doesn't usually speak with words. Instead, it speaks with pokes and nudges and tickles and delight. We can choose to listen to our inner voice, even if it isn't clear yet. And to our friends and family we can simply say, "I'm taking care of something important."

There is a stirring deep inside me, an energy trying to get my attention. It is tugging at me like a child pulling my shirttails asking me to see something important. When I give it my attention, it feels right and necessary. I'm going to explore this new idea, this new part of me, with loving curiosity. And I'm okay with not being able to explain it to anyone else.

Practice listening to your intuition,
your inner voice; ask questions;
be curious;
see what you see; hear what you hear;
and then act upon what you know to be true.

—CLARISSA PINKOLA ESTES

47.

We can all benefit from having a *Board of Direction* in life. These may be people we know or inspiring strangers who are out there doing the things we want to be doing. Identifying and reaching out to potential mentors has never been easier than it is today. And though some movers and shakers may be too busy to respond to a request for a few minutes of their time, there are many role models around us who are willing, and even eager, to share their wisdom.

I recognize that I'm not the first person to walk this path; many others have been where I am and have gone where I want to go. I will seek out those inspiring souls who have already risen to the top and I will learn from their guidance and wisdom. I don't have to reinvent the wheel. I just have to ask for help.

If I have seen further
it is by standing on the shoulders of giants.

—ISAAC NEWTON

48.

Learning to sit with discomfort is one of the most loving things we can do while reinventing ourselves. "New" is almost always uncomfortable, and when learning to show up in new ways, we'll most certainly experience discomfort. If we interpret this sensation as our comfort zone being stretched, we'll be less likely to resist it. As our comfort zone expands, we gain the confidence to step past this boundary and find the freedom that lives on the other side.

I'm okay with feeling the discomfort that comes along with being on my path. I understand that this tension in my body is my ego trying to protect me from change. But change is what I seek; therefore, I must seek these uncomfortable moments also. I choose to sit quietly and feel the sensations in my body. The longer I sit with myself, the less power the discomfort has over me.

The more you practice tolerating discomfort,
the more confidence you'll gain
in your ability to accept new challenges.

—AMY MORIN

49.

We often procrastinate when making important changes in life because we don't yet feel confident about our ability to do so. But confidence is not what it takes to begin—courage is. *Courage* is the willingness to face our fears and to step into the unknown. It is our readiness to sit with our own discomfort and do the hard work necessary to manifest new outcomes. *Confidence* can only grow when we practice courage long enough.

I am being courageous every time I . . . try something new; try something for which I have no known talent; risk being rejected, ignored, or embarrassed; attempt to right a wrong; set out to do something alone; follow my instincts; leave the known in search of the unknown; tell someone no; ask someone to believe in me; open my heart to love; fall down and get back up again; trust. Confidence is the reward I receive for mastering my courage.

You cannot swim for new horizons
until you have courage to lose sight of the shore.

—WILLIAM FAULKNER

50.

Sometimes we pick a destination for our journey because of the rewards it could bring. But if the journey itself is not rewarding, then the outcome is more likely to be disappointing when we don't end up with the exact results we had hoped for. On the other hand, when we choose our journey based on the fulfillment we receive on the path itself, even unexpected destinations are more likely to delight us.

When I spend my time and energy engaged in the activities that nourish me, instead of chasing after outcomes I wish I could accomplish, paths open up that reveal fulfilling opportunities I wouldn't otherwise have imagined.

Let the beauty we love be what we do.

—RUMI

51.

It's easy to place conditions on our well-being. We tell ourselves, "If I achieve this outcome, I'll feel good. And if I don't, then I won't." In the end, this *conditional mindset* paralyzes us, preventing us from taking action because we're afraid we'll make the wrong choices along the way. Instead, we can practice *unconditional well-being*, allowing ourselves to feel whole, worthy, and content, regardless of outcome. Freedom comes when we learn to trust our ability to follow the flow of unfolding events and still feel the essence of our well-being.

I have many choices for how to move forward in this moment and I trust that regardless of the choices I make, I'll be just fine. I can navigate any uncertainty I feel, knowing that everything I'm looking for already exists within me. My journey is simply about finding the right outlet for the expression of myself.

The truth is, everything will be okay
as soon as you are okay with everything.

—MICHAEL A. SINGER

52.

Personal reinvention can feel overwhelming because it implies the necessity for massive change. But reinventing yourself doesn't mean you have to disassemble your life to build something new from the pieces. You don't have to quit your job, or abandon your relationships, or move to Paris. Reinvention involves becoming deeply curious about what makes you come alive and learning to incorporate more of those experiences into your daily life. Small changes can make a big difference when you engage in activities you look forward to each day.

I choose not to send my castle tumbling down—I have responsibilities to those inside. But I can carve windows in walls, allowing the sunlight to permeate my kingdom. I don't have to remove the darkness; I just have to allow the light.

Follow your bliss
and don't be afraid, and doors will open
where you didn't know they were going to be.

—JOSEPH CAMPBELL

53.

Desiring big changes in life can make us feel like a child peering off the edge of a diving board for the first time—it's scary. But like a child, we can opt out of the high dive and choose instead to take *small dives*, which are opportunities to be in action in small ways. Taking a class, planning a workshop, organizing an event, or starting a blog are examples of ways to be in action in the arena of our dreams. Small dives get us into the pool, where we'll soon realize it's not as scary as we thought.

When I find small ways to dive into my goals, I give myself the opportunity to stretch my comfort zone, try on a new identity for size, be in contact with like-minded people, and learn what works and doesn't work. I go from being a person who wants to do something special, to being a person who is doing something special.

Life is a travelling to the edge of knowledge, then a leap taken.

—D. H. LAWRENCE

54.

When seeking to reinvent ourselves, we can take valuable cues from the product design industry. *Design thinking* seeks to solve complex problems through a process of ideation and exploration. Rather than being attached to a particular outcome, designers try to test as many creative ideas as possible before deciding on the final product design. We can follow their lead when it comes to redesigning ourselves. When we allow our process to be more about exploration than expectation, we set ourselves up for the greatest number of options and the best possible chance for success.

When I let my curiosity take the lead, I allow creativity to guide my process of becoming. Through my exploration, I get to know myself better and I discover there's more than one path toward fulfillment. Through my experimentation, I get to try each path until I find the one that works the best.

Just as established products and brands
need updating to stay alive and vibrant,
you periodically need to
refresh and reinvent yourself.

—MIREILLE GUILIANO

55.

Many of us turn to personal reinvention hoping to create more *flow* in our lives. Flow happens when we overcome resistance, enabling life to become effortless and joyful. People often resort to drugs or alcohol to generate a temporary illusion of flow, but we can create this experience in a healthy way that lasts. The key to experiencing flow is practicing meaningful but difficult activities repeatedly, until they're no longer difficult. Training our bodies and brains to do hard things allows us to get *lost* in the doing while experiencing the *joy* of the doing.

Change is hard, and in the past I've been critical of myself for not being strong enough to face the hard parts. But I'm now able to see that learning to do these challenging things is the objective of my transformation process. The more I practice doing hard things, the less difficult they become and the more I enjoy the process.

Most enjoyable activities are not natural;
they demand an effort
that initially one is reluctant to make.
But once the interaction starts to provide feedback to the person's skills,
it usually begins to be intrinsically rewarding.

—MIHALY CSIKSZENTMIHALYI

56.

On our journey toward our True Self, attention must be paid to our *gifts*—our mysterious, idiosyncratic fascinations. Our gifts appear in the themes and activities in which we lose ourselves for hours, slipping into a delicious state of effortless flow. But what may seem like an indulgence is so much more. Our gifts are the fuel for our spirit and the beckoning gateway to our *aliveness*. Honoring our gifts allows us to show up fully in life, both for ourselves and for those we love.

My gifts are part of the beauty of my uniqueness. When I honor and celebrate these facets of myself, I uplift not only myself, but those around me as well. My energy is contagious, and I choose to spread joy. The more I play with my delight, the more I learn about how I'd like to interact with the world in the future.

We can take no credit for our gifts.
It's what we do with them that matters.

—MARY BURCHELL

57.

When we learn that our gifts can be applied toward solving problems in the world around us and we feel pulled toward this action, we discover our *callings*. These callings are a gift upon a gift—engaging in them feels like a gift to ourselves, but they also become a gift we give for the benefit of others. Pursuing our callings may feel like a deviation from our official narrative, but when we look closely at our lifelong journey, we'll often discover that the signs have been pointing us in this direction all along.

When I apply my gifts toward bettering the world around me, my heart expands to contain more love, more joy, and more appreciation. Though I couldn't pursue this path in the past, I'm feeling called to reconsider it now. My gifts are needed, and it's my honor to contribute.

The purpose of life is to discover your gift.
The work of life is to develop it.
The meaning of life is to give your gift away.

—DAVID S. VISCOTT

58.

Organization experts recommend that we clean our closets before shopping for new clothes, because they know that what we go in search of, we often already possess. Similarly, taking a *gratitude inventory* of all the aspects of our life and identity that we cherish can help refine or reframe our desire for change. Studies show that consistently practicing gratitude contributes to a greater sense of happiness and well-being, which can give us clarity about our reinvention process. Desiring more in life is wonderful as long as we are aware and appreciative of what we already have.

When I take the time to view everything in my life I would be sad to lose, I become aware of all I have that I'm grateful for. When I'm aware of my abundance, I'm less governed by a sense of scarcity. When I'm less focused on what I don't have, I can focus more on what I want with a sense of optimism and joy.

We can only be said
to be alive in those moments
when our hearts are conscious of our treasure.

—THORNTON WILDER

59.

One of the best ways to move forward in life is to clear a path—literally. Clutter not only wastes space, it also wastes mental energy. Having too much *stuff* around you creates the unconscious sensation of having too many choices to make, which can lead you to feeling discouraged without even knowing why. If you feel plagued by indecision or "analysis paralysis" in your daily life, try getting rid of things in your physical space that no longer serve you. You may be surprised at how much easier it is to move forward toward other ambitions without the physical and mental clutter standing in your way.

As I scan the spaces where I spend my time, I notice that everything around me has a story attached to it. Many of these stories remind me of the expectations I had for the items as well as the memories I associate with them. I no longer feel the need to cling to artifacts that keep me held in the past. I now choose to move forward and let go of things that no longer serve a physical or emotional purpose in my life.

Get rid of clutter
and you may just find it was blocking the door
you've been looking for.

—KATRINA MAYER

60.

Contrary to what some people believe, *desire* is not a dirty word. In fact, our desire is as important to our survival as our heartbeat. Desire not only guides us toward food and love—things we need to survive—it also guides us toward ambitions and accomplishments, things we need to thrive. We begin to achieve freedom only when we stop shaming our desire. When we embrace desire for our greatest good, the path toward freedom mysteriously begins to appear before us.

My desires remind me of what's most important and necessary in life, and they give my life meaning at the deepest level. I understand that my desires help guide my thoughts, which guide my actions, which guide my outcomes. My desires are the seed level of my experiences in life.

I prefer to be a dreamer among the humblest,
with visions to be realized,
than lord among those
without dreams and desires.

—KAHLIL GIBRAN

61.

Sometimes we're afraid to acknowledge our desires because they trigger negative emotions. We may fear disappointment or feel guilty for wanting more than we believe we deserve. When we try to snuff out our desires, like fingers over a match, we don't make the desires go away, we just burn our fingers. Desires are precious and worthy, even under painful circumstances. When life hands us difficult situations, it is our desires that will pave a path through them. The path may not be the one we planned, but desire will find a way to move us in the right direction.

I have a desire for something that may be improbable at this point in my life. But that doesn't mean my desire isn't meaningful or that it can't help lead me toward greater joy and satisfaction. I choose to honor my desire and listen to what it has to share with me. My desire will give me clues about changes I can make to bring more of what I want into my life.

It is our wounds that create in us a desire to
reach for miracles.
The fulfillment of such miracles
depends on whether
we let our wounds pull us down
or lift us up towards our dreams.

—JOCELYN SORIANO

62.

Many of us hold *core beliefs* that are in opposition to our path. These deeply held assumptions about ourselves and the world, handed down to us by our families and our communities, often contain ideologies about what is and isn't possible for us. Navigating the inner conflict caused by these self-defeating beliefs is like trying to drive with the emergency brake on—we'll move forward, but very slowly and with great resistance. When our core beliefs become obstacles to creating positive change, a trained therapist or counselor can help us separate the beliefs of others from our own, which is the first step toward reinventing our thinking.

I know my family and community meant well when they passed along their beliefs, but I'm learning now that many of these beliefs aren't truths. I've come to realize that some of these beliefs no longer serve me, and I'm ready to let them go. I will find the support I need to release these limiting thoughts so I can move forward toward a life that inspires me.

To accomplish great things we must not only act,
but also dream;
not only plan, but also believe.

—ANATOLE FRANCE

63.

Within each of us exists an *inner security guard*. This character is the voice of our self-criticism and fear, brilliantly masked as a vital protector of our well-being. Our inner security guard is a hard-wired remnant of our biological safety instinct and it has one mission—to keep us safe. It doesn't care if we live boring, monotonous lives, so long as we don't take risks. But risks are required for personal growth and fulfillment. So while we may not be able to get rid of our inner security guard, when we hear it sounding another false alarm, we can give it some decaf coffee and ask it to relax.

Dear Inner Security Guard, I recognize that you're a hard worker and you take pride in your job. But I'd like to point out that you pulled the fire alarm three times this week just because I turned up the heat with my endeavors. You're a vital part of our operation, but I need to ask you to chill out a bit so I can get some work done.

Playing it safe requires
that we avoid risky situations—
which covers pretty much all of life.

—TARA BRACH

64.

One of the best tools we have for creative solutions to our complex challenges is . . . sleep! Though it may seem like staying up extra late and getting up extra early helps our productivity, research has shown that being deprived of sleep has a dramatic negative impact on memory, judgement, creativity, and mood. Sleep is when the brain forms neurological connections that are vital to thinking and learning. When assembling the grand jigsaw puzzle that is our life in progress, sleep is the glue that holds it all together.

Lullaby and goodnight, I'll dream about my own delight. When I fade, my thoughts unwind, as slumber gently boosts my mind. While I sleep, my dreams renew, bringing strength to days anew. When I wake, clear and bright, my dreams are ready to take flight.

It is a common experience
that a problem difficult at night
is resolved in the morning
after the committee of sleep has worked on it.

—JOHN STEINBECK

65.

Many of us set out on the personal reinvention trail excited and full of motivation, so it's easy to expect that we should get where we're going quickly. But personal transformation is a marathon, not a sprint. There are many clues along the trail that will help us get where we need to go, and if we run too fast we may miss them. Taking the time to process the thoughts, emotions, and experiences we encounter along the way will help us pick the right path and pivot when needed.

When I catch myself thinking that I should have reached the finish line already, I remind myself that there is no finish line. There is only the direction I want to travel, mile markers, and amazing places of interest. As I gain clarity, the path becomes clearer and the journey becomes more enjoyable.

Our happiest moments as tourists
seem to be when we stumble upon one thing
while in pursuit of something else.

—LAWRENCE BLOCK

66.

If you find yourself on the personal reinvention treadmill but not making progress, take a moment to distinguish between *what you want now* and *what you want most*. If *what you want now* involves immediate gratification, you're likely to go in circles to satisfy your cravings. When you focus on *what you want most*, which usually involves lasting satisfaction, it's easier to break down the necessary steps to get there. When *what you want now* is to take these necessary steps, you get off the treadmill and start making genuine progress.

I'm aware of my cravings in this moment,
and I recognize that giving in to them
won't make me happier in the long run.
These cravings represent my small desires,
but what I'm really hungry for are my big
desires. I will sit quietly with the discomfort
of my superficial urges until they pass, and
then I will get busy on the activities that are
truly meaningful for me.

To say no when you need to say no,
and yes when you need to say yes,
you need a third power:
the ability to remember what you really want.

—KELLY MCGONIGAL

67.

Creating *what you want most* in life is a lot like preparing to cook a special dinner. You can't just hope for this amazing meal to magically appear; you have to plan for it. You'll want to research recipes and ingredients, inventory what you do and don't already have in your kitchen, make a list of everything you need to buy, and create a timeline so you know when to begin. Then you'll go through the process of following the steps you've laid out for getting from start to finish. Creating *what you want most* in life is no different. It requires thoughtful research, planning, and consistent action to make it happen.

Recipe for success in life: Combine equal parts Imagination, Creativity, Organization, Accountability, Clarity, Ambition, Spontaneity, and Joy. Simmer over constant heat. Allow to thicken; add spice as necessary. Top with your favorite hot sauce. Serve on your best china. Share with friends and loved ones.

This is my invariable advice to people:
Learn how to cook—try new recipes,
learn from your mistakes,
be fearless, and above all have fun!

—JULIA CHILD

68.

Imagine you're going on a treasure hunt. You wouldn't start wandering in any direction. You'd first consult your treasure map and then select your actions mindfully and with purpose. Your personal reinvention journey requires this same energy, so it's important to master *mindful mornings*. Morning is our best opportunity to start fresh and select our intentions and attitudes for the day. We can envision *what we want most* and review our steps to get there. Most of all, we can ensure that our *autopilot*—old habits, behaviors, and disempowering beliefs—doesn't take us backward on

our treasure hunt.

Today is a new day and a new beginning. I'm open and eager for all that awaits me. Today I get to choose my thoughts and my actions. I will imagine the ways in which my day may play out, and I will plan my empowered approach to the scenarios I may encounter. Today I'm looking forward to my journey.

> You can't go back and make a new start,
> but you can start right now
> and make a brand new ending.

—JAMES R. SHERMAN

69.

When we fill all our available time with *doing* so we can feel productive and worthy, we find ourselves afflicted with *busy-bee syndrome.* The "buzz" we get distracts us from the awareness that something important is missing from our lives. It gives us an excuse for not having to address our soul's longing—because, well, we just don't have the time! Purging our lives of low-priority tasks and obligations, when possible, frees up time and space for us to explore new horizons and contributes to our well-being.

I have been led to believe that hard work and sacrifice = worthiness = happiness. But somehow my accomplishments haven't resulted in the happiness I sought. Rather than running in circles to feel worthy, I choose to search for the activities that ignite my spirit. I'm now aware that I can work hard when it's required and still find time to nourish my soul.

Don't get so busy making a living
that you forget to make a life.

—DOLLY PARTON

70.

We live in a world that provides a constant stream of stimulation, ensuring we never need to experience boredom. But boredom is the *gateway to self-discovery*. Your process of personal reinvention requires time to sit quietly and be curious about the world around you. Rather than defaulting to devices and distractions during idle moments, look around with curiosity and observe the people, things, and situations that capture your attention. The more you notice the world around you, the more deeply you'll experience the world within you.

I'm becoming aware of all the times I feel compelled to check my phone—in the grocery line, waiting in the car, sitting at a traffic light, in the bathroom. . . . I recognize that I'm responding to the discomfort of sitting still. But sitting still is a magical space for thoughts, ideas, and intuition. The next time I feel the urge to be entertained, I'll do it the old-fashioned way—by observing the world around me.

> You need to let the little things
> that would ordinarily bore you
> suddenly thrill you.
>
> —ANDY WARHOL

71.

We all have different beliefs about how the world works, but most of us, at one time or another, have encountered coincidences, synchronicities, and unexplainable good fortune. When the "stars align" in mysterious ways, we can easily say that *magic is afoot* and the *Divine* is acting on our behalf. But when negative and undesirable things happen, it may also be that the stars are aligning for us. Sometimes, a door has to close first before another door can open, leading us in a better direction. When we're faced with seemingly negative events, we can still ask if perhaps *magic is afoot,* clearing the way for something better in the future.

I may not be happy with the way certain events are playing out, but I must ask—what if something's being orchestrated behind the scenes to help me in ways I can't yet understand? I imagine my future self might say to me, "One day this will all make sense. Please be patient and trust."

I am open to the guidance of synchronicity, and do not let expectations hinder my path.

—(ATTRIBUTED TO) THE DALAI LAMA

72.

Whatever our personal beliefs may be, faith is a powerful force that acknowledges the unseen order of things. The known and unknown world around us works in ways we can't fully understand. But we can have faith that we have always been part of a grander plan for our own personal growth. When we hold the belief that the Universe has our best interests at heart and that unseen forces will meet us halfway to provide the support we need, we gather the courage necessary to step into the unknown.

Just as the seed has no idea that a gardener has planted it and is caring for its growth, I cannot know what unseen force is overseeing my own natural emergence. But I can have faith that I am part of a miraculous system that will provide me with the support I need to blossom. Every day I will remind myself, though I cannot see the grander picture, the future is unfolding in the best possible way.

Faith is the daring of the soul
to go farther than it can see.

—WILLIAM NEWTON CLARKE

73.

We don't need to be religious to understand that personal prayer is a powerful tool. Prayer is a declaration that we are committed to our journey and it allows us to be open to the unknown path ahead. When we offer our intentions to the Universe and ask for support in return, we clarify our desires, both for ourselves and for the Higher Powers around us which may be listening. Whether we've already developed a relationship with the Unknown, or we're sharing our desires for the first time, prayer brings us closer to our desired reality.

I give thanks for all the beauty, love, and joy that surrounds me. In this moment, I ask for the strength and courage to do what I must to transform myself. Please help me to notice those moments when I'm being pulled back into old habits that don't serve me. And please help me to see the big and beautiful picture that is my potential. Thank you for the opportunity to be on this quest, and to be a role model for those who are still struggling to begin theirs.

> Prayer is not asking.
> It is a longing of the soul.
>
> —MAHATMA GANDHI

74.

As children, we were taught that someone would always come to save the day. We turned to superheroes for inspiration and revelation. As adults, we see heroes all around us—people we admire who are engaged in extraordinary acts we find meaningful. But who says we need to sit on the sidelines and simply admire exceptional characters embodying the qualities we value? When we decide to be more than a spectator and make the choice to embody these same remarkable characteristics, we *become our own heroes*, and we bridge the gap between the life we're living and the life we'd like to be living.

I choose to embody the qualities of those inspiring souls who are engaged in extraordinary lives. I will seek opportunities to align myself with their example in ways that bring me closer to my goals. I no longer have to look outside myself for inspiration; I will now look inside myself.

We do not have to become heroes overnight.
Just a step at a time,
meeting each thing that comes up . . .
discovering we have the strength
to stare it down.

—ELEANOR ROOSEVELT

75.

Beware the perils of *people-pleasing*. Seeking positive feedback from others can cause us to say yes to things that don't benefit us or aren't aligned with our goals. Even though it feels good to be seen favorably by other people, seeking to please others puts us at risk for sacrificing our own interests in favor of theirs. Saying no may be uncomfortable; we may even lose friends because of it. But if they're the people who are preventing us from becoming the person we want to be, we're better off finding better friends who will embrace and support our journeys.

Dear Younger Me: I'm older and wiser now and I've learned that by going out of our way to make other people happy, we're doing what's best for them, not for us. I know it's hard to make choices and decisions that go against the grain, and yes, there will be times when we feel lonely because of it. But I'm here to tell you that those will be some of the best choices we make in life, and eventually we'll be surrounded by people who support our journey.

People pleasing pleases everyone but the pleaser.

—SANJO JENDAYI

76.

For many of us, *perfectionism* is a tactic for avoiding failure and any experiences that threaten our sense of identity and worthiness. But perfectionism doesn't protect us from failure; it actually ensures it. Perfectionism prevents us from attempting anything for which success isn't guaranteed. And since the path forward is paved with uncertainty, perfectionism ensures we don't move forward. *Imperfection*, on the other hand, is a key to happiness and success because it opens the door to a wide variety of experiences that allow us to learn, grow, and achieve.

I often use perfectionism to avoid life's prickly parts—those uncomfortable experiences I interpret to mean there's something wrong with me. But I'm learning to see these prickly parts as simply the boundaries of my comfort zone, and they're a beautiful signal that I'm stepping into the realm of my personal growth and transformation.

Perfection is a twenty-ton shield
that we lug around thinking it will protect us
when in fact, it's the thing
that's really preventing us
from taking flight.

—BRENÉ BROWN

77.

We sell ourselves short when we fall into a *fixed mindset*—the belief that "we are who we are" and we're not likely to change. Our fixed mindset says things like, "I'm not smart enough to figure this out," or "If I put myself out there, people will discover all my shortcomings." Instead, adopting a *growth mindset* allows us to experience what science has already discovered—that by working hard at challenging tasks, we actually grow new brain cells and we do indeed become smarter and more skilled. A growth mindset encourages self-talk like, "I haven't figured out how to do this *yet*," and "If I put myself out there, I'll learn what I need to know along the way."

When I feel stuck and defeated, I remind myself that I'm a work in progress and I'm learning. Every opportunity I have to move past self-defeating thoughts is an opportunity to rewrite the story of my life. My growth mindset reminds me that I'm not skilled at this process, yet. I'm not able to accomplish these things, yet. I'm not the person I want to be, yet. But I will be soon.

In one world, the world of fixed traits,
success is about proving
you're smart or talented.
Validating yourself. In the other,
the world of changing qualities,
it's about stretching yourself
to learn something new. Developing yourself.

—CAROL DWECK

78.

Sometimes life-altering events can send our world tumbling down, causing us to experience emotional distress. But when we allow traumatic life experiences to open the door to empathy, compassion, and appreciation, we may find a renewed sense of purpose on the other side. This *post-traumatic growth* allows us to see our role in the world in a new light, giving us the opportunity to reinvent ourselves for the better as a result. This new state of being doesn't mean that our trauma was good; it simply means that something good has come from it.

I cannot know why my life has taken the turn it has, but I do know that my trauma has become my teacher. I've learned to develop inner resources that I wouldn't have found otherwise, and I've discovered new and meaningful connections with others who have experienced similar circumstances. I know now that sharing my process of growth with those who are struggling fills me with a sense of purpose and hope, and I'm beginning to feel whole again.

Opportunities to find
deeper powers within ourselves
come when life seems most challenging.

—JOSEPH CAMPBELL

79.

As we learn and internalize the skills and strat-egies for reinventing ourselves, we should be reminded that we learn best what we teach to others. Finding opportunities to mentor those who are on a similar path allows us to learn and embody concepts at a deeper level. When we apply these ideas outside of ourselves, we gain a more profound awareness of how they apply inside our own experience. Showing generosity of spirit by supporting others, in turn, supports our own spirit of growth. And the compassion we feel for another who is struggling is the same compassion we can direct toward ourselves, to encourage our own process.

I have the desire, time, and willingness to pass on what I have learned to others. I also know that I will learn from those I teach. What has come to me is meant to be shared, and what I share will come back to me.

While we teach, we learn.

—SENECA

80.

Personal reinvention doesn't happen overnight. Instead, we find that we must reinvent ourselves every day, until our new selves become second nature. To make this process easier, we can reduce the burden of daily decision-making by cultivating *positive habits*. To do this, we can identify the activities our "future self" would engage in, and find short-term, immediate rewards for making those activities part of our daily routine. Over time, we won't need the rewards anymore—the gratification of becoming the person who engages with life in this way will be all the reward we need.

If my life were a movie and I were the hero, I would have a sidekick: Trusty Habits. My Trusty Habits would help me disempower distractions in a single bound, dismantle friction in a flash, and clear the way for the hero (that's me!) to focus on the important business at hand. The more I allow my Trusty Habits to guide my choices throughout the day, the more I become aligned with the hero I want to be.

We become what we repeatedly do.

—ARISTOTLE

81.

Every road trip deserves its own playlist, and so does our journey of reinvention. Think back to a time in your life when you experienced optimism, empowerment, and joy. Do you remember the music you were listening to at that time? Put the same music on today, and you're likely to experience those same emotions. Neuroscience has shown that music activates parts of the brain that are integral to our thriving—it enhances critical thinking, communication, confidence, and hope. Whether it's music from your past or modern anthems that motivate, an *inspiring playlist* is like high-octane fuel for your personal journey.

Music goes deeper than my mind and communicates with my soul. It reminds me of who I am at my core and encourages me to tap into my internal resources. I've chosen the soundtrack for my journey thoughtfully and consider it my ally on this path. When I begin to lose steam, this music stokes the fire within to keep me moving forward.

Music is the language of the spirit.
It opens the secret of life,
bringing peace, abolishing strife.

—KAHLIL GIBRAN

82.

When we assume new roles and enter new spaces in life, it's easy to convince ourselves that we don't really belong here. We experience *imposter syndrome* when we feel out of place or out of our league, and fear being discovered as a fraud. This self-sabotaging belief can cause us to deny our dreams and abandon our ambitions. However, feeling like an imposter doesn't mean we don't belong where we are; it simply means we're in the process of developing our confidence in this arena. Our path has led us to where we are, and we'll continue to move forward as we learn, grow, and improve.

Sometimes I catch myself feeling small and out of place in my surroundings. When I confide in a friend or peer, I'm often surprised to learn that they also experience similar insecurities. I remind myself that having made it this far is evidence enough that I belong here. I choose to learn from those who have been where I am, and I choose to support those who are where I once was.

Do not let what you cannot do interfere with what you can do.

—JOHN WOODEN

83.

Fear is what we experience when we anticipate suffering in the future, and it has the power to make us abandon well-intentioned goals. But the suffering we feel in *response* to our fear is usually greater than the discomfort of actually navigating the challenging situation itself. We can begin to make peace with our fear by acknowledging it for what it really is—a response to a hypothetical situation. Then we can disempower our fear by reminding ourselves that our *fear of suffering* is usually worse than the uncomfortable experiences we're avoiding.

My fear accompanies me like an unwanted imaginary friend. At times it helps keep me safe, but more often it just sits behind me and kicks the back of my chair. I don't have to be afraid of my fear; it's a consolation prize for being human. I can simply acknowledge it, thank it for its concern, and continue making progress toward my goals.

We suffer more often
in imagination than in reality.

—SENECA

84.

Fear often keeps us stuck because there's a *reward* in it for us—the prize of predictability and security. By avoiding the unknown, we ensure that life continues to look the same, and change doesn't rock the boat. But this doesn't work so well when we're on a journey toward personal transformation, which requires change. To release the grasp that fear has on us, we have to realize there's an even greater reward for facing and overcoming it. Our reward is everything that opens up for us that previously wasn't possible.

When fear and "what-ifs" dominate my thinking, I can simply ask, "What would be possible for me if I were no longer afraid of this?" In the space left after removing my fear, I can begin to see clearly what I have to gain by stepping out of my comfort zone. In the end, I realize that the discomfort of my life staying the same is greater than the discomfort of facing my fear.

> Never let the fear of striking out
> keep you from playing the game.
>
> —BABE RUTH

85.

Setting out on a journey of transformation can feel like a daunting task. If we don't see examples of courageous people on similar journeys around us, we can find inspiration by connecting with the characters in inspiring movies. Stories portraying the Hero's Journey follow characters who must overcome adversity through perseverance and growth. These characters reflect the human condition—they're a reflection of us. Compiling a list of triumphant movies and planning regular movie nights can help us muster strength when we need it most.

As a child, I felt invincible because the characters in the movies I adored were themselves invincible. Because I felt invincible, indeed it seemed to be true. Today I realize that little has changed. When I approach the world around me from a place of invincibility, the world seems to respond in kind, allowing me often to triumph in my endeavors.

Believe in yourself
and there will come a day
when others will have
no choice but to believe with you.

—MUFASA (FROM *THE LION KING*)

86.

Many of us are seeking personal reinvention to shift from a place of feeling fractured to a place of feeling whole. We become fractured when the *self* we reveal to others is different from the *self* we know ourselves to be. We can begin to reconcile our inner and outer worlds when we stop letting other people's opinions be the criteria for valuing ourselves. Letting go of the need to make others comfortable with our presence gives us the space necessary to heal our fractures. By celebrating our own uniqueness and allowing our hidden selves to be seen, we create the path to wholeness.

I realize that I have been looking at myself through other people's eyes, working hard to meet their expectations. I now know that I have far more to offer than the limited roles they've assigned me. I no longer feel obligated to show up in ways they find pleasing. Instead I will show up as myself and let them get to know the true essence of who I am.

Your job, throughout your entire life,
is to disappoint as many people as it takes
to avoid disappointing yourself.

—GLENNON DOYLE

87.

Our personal reinvention is bound to become frustrating when we set expectations that are rigid and uncompromising. When our endeavors don't make us feel the way we expect, when people don't respond the way we expect, or when our projects don't yield the amount of money or fame we expect, we can fall into a victim mindset. Learning to do new things and show up in new ways is exactly that—learning. Our outcomes are simply a bonus feature of the experience.

In those moments when I feel the heat rising in my body because my efforts are being met with resistance, I will encourage myself to approach my endeavors with a sense of curiosity, rather than attachment. I will be gentle with myself, and I will remember that there are many paths toward my destination. In hindsight, I will know that everything is playing out exactly as it is meant to.

Expectation is the root of all heartache.

—ANONYMOUS

88.

Breath work is a secret passageway into our inner world. When we focus on our breath, we learn to tune out the distractions that pull our attention away from our personal journeys. Breathing slowly and intentionally calms the nervous system, relieves anxiety, and allows us to remember our values and goals. Setting aside a few minutes every day to sit quietly and count our inhales and exhales will help to develop our quality of attention and prepare us to engage with our goals in an empowered way.

Taking time to consciously sit and breathe is a gift I give to myself. When I close my eyes and inhale for five counts—one, two, three, four, five—hold my breath for two counts—one, two—slowly exhale for ten counts—one, two, three, four, five, six, seven, eight, nine, ten—hold for two counts—one, two—and repeat, I find that the noise from the world around me slowly disappears. Over time, my quiet, wise, inner voice percolates up to provide me valuable guidance.

Breathe and you dwell in the here and now.

—THICH NHAT HANH

89.

It's important to incorporate more fun into our days! Fun isn't just about giving ourselves a break; fun and play are important ways to spark creativity and to experiment with new interests. Studies have shown that engaging in play actually stimulates neural connections in the problem-solving regions of the brain, allowing us to consider more possibilities than if we only engage in routine activities. Play is also known to relieve stress, improve relationships, and add energy and vitality to our lives. Finding more ways to bring play into our days can actually help us make faster progress toward our goals.

When I make time for fun and play, for no other reason than exploring my own joy and vitality, I open up pathways in my mind that hold secrets and answers to some of my biggest questions. Play is not frivolous and it's not selfish—it allows me to grow into the best and most productive version of myself.

Play lies at the core of creativity and innovation.

—STUART BROWN

90.

As we navigate daily life, we occasionally encounter *nudges*. These are experiences that get our attention, gently asking us if we want to move in a new direction. Our nudges are subtle wake-up calls, hinting to us that something different is possible. They ask us to imagine ourselves interacting with the world in new ways. Nudges are wonderful gifts, and when we begin to pay attention to them, we'll probably notice a pattern. We don't necessarily have to say yes to every invitation to make a change in our lives, but if nudges show up repeatedly, we can honor them with our attention and curiosity.

When I encounter ideas that ask me to play with them, I will say yes, even if only for a moment. I will ask these ideas if they have a message for me, and if they do, I will consider it a gift. After I have considered these ideas, I may choose to put them away, but I may also invite them to come back and play again sometime.

Nothing comes unannounced,
but many can miss the announcement.
So it's very important to actually listen
to your own intuition
rather than driving through it.

—TERENCE MCKENNA

91.

When change isn't happening because we're stuck in a comfort zone, we may need a push to move us forward. A *push* may come in the form of an unexpected opportunity or a sudden detour that shifts the boundaries of our comfort and moves us further and faster than we would have gone on our own. Pushes often create an uncomfortable momentum, but they can also clear a remarkable path for personal growth.

The next time you feel like a challenging event is happening *to* you, ask if perhaps a push is allowing it to happen *for* you.

When change forces me out of my routine, it can feel like I'm being pushed into a river. I may have to work hard to swim against the rushing current, but once I relax into the experience, I often notice the current is carrying me in a direction I'd actually like to go.

If someone offers you an amazing opportunity, but you are not sure you can do it, say yes—then learn how to do it later.

—RICHARD BRANSON

92.

Cows, goats, and sheep are known as "ruminants" because they chew their food over and over, all day long, so it can be digested, which consumes most of their time and energy. We humans also ruminate, spending our time chewing on what's wrong or missing from our lives, trying to figure out why it's wrong and what's so wrong about it.

If you find yourself spending precious time and energy focused on the absence of what you desire, consider that this kind of thinking may not be helpful. Then give yourself a rest by shifting your attention to the inspiring people and ideas that align with the life you want to create.

Sometimes my thoughts fixate on what is wrong with my present situation. But I know that where my mind goes, my energy flows. I choose not to feed negativity. I choose instead to feed and focus on my wishes, dreams, hopes, and aspirations. I choose to celebrate my desires and the life I'm creating.

Shift your attention, and your emotion shifts.
Shift your emotion, and your attention shifts.

—FREDERICK DODSON

93.

Science has shown that our thoughts, in the form of electricity moving through neural pathways in the brain, travel at speeds up to 120 meters per second. So claiming that our thoughts are racing is no exaggeration! When we find ourselves overwhelmed by racing or repetitive thoughts, we can use *journaling* as a tool to slow down our minds and expand our awareness. Putting our thoughts on paper helps us identify the themes and interests that captivate our attention and allows us to make sense of them in a meaningful way.

When I give my thoughts a voice, and witness them without judgement, I can see the parts of myself that are desiring to be heard. By allowing my fear to have a voice, I can see it clearly and acknowledge it for trying to keep me safe. By allowing my wisdom to have a voice, I can see that the answers I seek are already within me.

Journaling is like whispering to one's self and listening at the same time.

—MINA MURRAY (IN *DRACULA*)

94.

People are often surprised to find out that *fear* and *excitement* originate in the same part of the brain—they're two sides of the same "stress" coin. When we feel fearful, we're interpreting our stress as negative. When we feel excited, we're interpreting our stress as positive. Fear and excitement both produce similar sensations in the body, thanks to the release of hormones, including adrenaline, cortisol, and dopamine, which can cause us to feel anxious. Choosing to interpret our stressful experiences as exciting opportunities for growth allows us to benefit from this brain-boosting cocktail of hormones and empowers us to reach our potential.

When I get to the edge of my comfort zone, I begin to feel fearful about the uncertainty of the unknown. But I can shift my fear into excitement by choosing to see the situation more as an opportunity than a threat. Embracing this experience as an adventure with great rewards to be had allows me to transform my anxiety into useful energy and helps me to perform under pressure.

When you choose to view
your stress response as helpful,
you create the biology of courage.

—KELLY MCGONIGAL

95.

We may believe that *procrastination* is a productivity problem, but when we postpone taking action on important or meaningful tasks, it's usually because we're having trouble *managing negative emotions* around the task. Taking action toward personal change is bound to cause uncomfortable feelings, but avoiding necessary tasks is likely to increase discomfort, not decrease it. When we choose to follow through on anxiety-inducing tasks, we'll find the resulting gratification to be much more satisfying than the superficial gratification we sought as a distraction.

When I'm faced with important tasks that I'd rather not do now, I can choose to think of them as "honey-dos" that I will complete with a sense of love and commitment for my future self. I imagine how pleased and appreciative my future self will be when I complete my tasks, and I choose to feel that pleasure and gratitude while taking action now.

A year from now
you may wish you had started today.

—ANONYMOUS

96.

If we put helium in a balloon but tie the balloon to the ground, the balloon won't rise. Likewise, if we fill ourselves with ideas, inspiration, education, and motivation, but we continue to weigh ourselves down with negative expectations and excuses for why our ideas won't work, we'll be destined to stay where we are.

In order to rise, you must be willing to let go of the self-defeating thoughts and fearful mindsets that keep you tied to the life you've been living. When you release the binding ties of your old patterns and limiting beliefs, you give your creativity a chance to soar.

During moments of lift, when I feel bound by heavy thoughts and feelings, I recognize that I have a choice—I can hold onto old ways of thinking that weigh me down, or I can take the risk that I'll be better off letting go of old patterns in favor of new ways of being. When I choose to let go, the horizon expands in front of me.

In order to grow, you must give up the struggle
to remain the same
and learn to embrace change at all times.

—MICHAEL A. SINGER

97.

Nobody has greater influence over the quality of our experiences than we do, so there's no relationship in our life more important than the one we have with ourselves. As we navigate our experiences, we engage in an ongoing internal dialog—one that can be either cruel or kind. Choosing to respond to unpredictable situations and inevitable disappointments with *self-compassion* means our self-love is unconditional and our sense of worthiness is no longer tied to outcomes or events. Responding to challenges with self-compassion stimulates creativity, encourages positive risk-taking, and generates more opportunities for the future.

I once believed I had to be hard on myself to be successful. I've since learned that harsh self-judgement causes suffering and leads me to play small, rather than play big. Approaching my experiences with self-compassion allows me to show up fully in life so I can continue creating, learning, growing, and achieving.

Love yourself first and everything else falls in line.
You really have to love yourself
to get anything done in this world.

—LUCILLE BALL

98.

When the chaos of the outer world imposes itself on our inner worlds, we can engage in self-care through *meditation*. This calming technique is not religious, though it can strengthen a religious practice. (There's an old saying, "Prayer is talking to God. Meditation is listening.") Meditation allows us to experience ourselves as we are, rooted in the present, without feeling the need to change or "improve" anything. Over time, we'll find our ability to focus is strengthened, while our inner awareness becomes more compassionate, loving, and receptive.

Meditation is the dance between my automatic thoughts and my purposeful focus. My focus leads the dance, and my thoughts are the partner. Every time my thoughts begin to lead, focus gently steps in to guide the dance. Both are important on the dance floor of my mind, but I am training my focus to set the tempo.

Meditation is a possibility
to awaken new dimensions within you.

—SADHGURU

99.

Tending to our personal growth is a lot like tending a garden. Preparing the soil for the process of creation often marks the end of one season, and the beginning of another. It requires hard work to clean out old debris and self-defeating beliefs that no longer serve us. Our wishes and desires are seeds containing the blueprints for all that will grow from our efforts. Once we plant our desires, we must care for and nourish them with positive emotions and consistent attention (and maybe a bit of "compost" from our old lives). Most of all, we must be patient, because tending a garden with new personal growth takes time.

I am a seed of potential, and Mother Earth
has blanketed me in her warmth and tucked
me into her comfort. It is dark here, but
I am encouraged to lie gently and just
be. With the passage of time, I grow and
expand. I peek through the heavy blankets
of earth to breathe in the air and feel the
sunshine. A new day begins that is fresh and
sweet.

A seed fears neither light nor darkness,
but uses both to grow.

—MATSHONA DHLIWAYO

100.

The only world that really exists for us is the one we see looking inward. It is through our inner world that we manifest our outer reality. Within the inner world, is a life-force that nourishes our spirits and enlivens our dreams. We have to feel our way through this world, becoming increasingly aware of the sensations that pull us in one direction or another. As we respond to these sensations, we have opportunities to make both small and large choices that are in alignment with our life-force and our true nature, choices that will guide the glorious nature of who we are to become.

My inner wisdom speaks to me through sensations of energy and excitement. I trust the messages I receive, and they help guide my choices and decisions. When my inner world and my outer world are aligned, I feel a sense of harmony and confidence, and I know I'm on the right path.

When you know who you are,
you will know how to act.

—STEPHEN COPE

101.

Our lives ebb and flow like the ocean, and we are surfers awaiting the waves. We sit, afloat, scanning the horizon until a distant ripple catches our eye. As the opportunity moves closer, we feel a strong desire to be part of it. We summon our energy and paddle like crazy to merge into the experience of it. Then we're on the wave of opportunity, traveling faster and further with a sense of aliveness we'd forgotten we could have. We ride this wave for as long as it allows . . . and just as swiftly as it welcomed us, it lets us go. Then we paddle back into the ocean of life to await the next transformative wave.

My reinvention process is never-ending, and that's what makes it so beautiful. With every curiosity I follow, every opportunity I embrace, and every adventure I embark upon, I find myself changed and transformed. I am still me, but I'm now more alert, more alive, and more grateful.

Our objective in life is to enjoy the process of allowing our True Self to emerge.

—KAREN SALITA

Karen Salita is a former competitive snow-boarder who reinvented herself as an industrial sales professional, enjoying close to twenty years of success in the field. While exploring the early years of midlife, she became intrigued by the process of personal transformation and began her next reinvention as an author. Karen writes about exploring one's deep potential in her blog, *Follow Your Wiggle*, at www.karensalita.com; on Instagram: karen.salita; and at Facebook.com/ FollowYourWiggle. Karen received a degree in communication studies from the University of Utah and now lives in Carson City, Nevada, with her sweetheart.

101 Soul Seeds

for Peacemakers & Justice Seekers

Authentic spirituality embeds us in the pain of the world and inspires commitment to social justice and conflict resolution. It seeks peace and justice in the public sphere, while nurturing a sense of connection with both God and all creation. Rooted in the deep mystery of Divine love, we can face challenges with confidence that God's vision of justice and peace will outlast the demagogues, dictators, and destroyers.

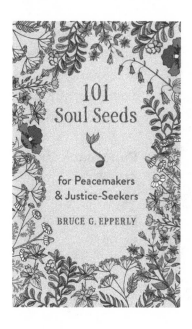

This book is intended to support your integration of peacemaking, justice-seeking, and spiritual growth.

Paperback Price: $12.99

Kindle Price: $4.99

101 Soul Seeds

for Parents of Adult Children

Being a parent held joys and challenges every step of the way, and never more so than when our children finally made it to adulthood. Now we can connect with them on deeper levels than ever—but unexpected potential pitfalls dot this new path we're traveling. *101 Soul Seeds for Parents of Adult Children* offers observations and quotes, coupled with simple prayers to help us navigate this portion of parenting . . . so we and our adult children grow closer to one another and closer to our own souls' destination.

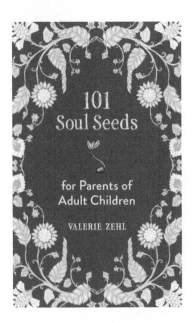

Paperback Price: $12.99

Kindle Price: $4.99

101 Soul Seeds

for Grandparents Working for a Better World

Grandparenting is truly a holy adventure. As we see and bring forth the inner divinity of our grandchildren, we have the opportunity to show them that they are not only our beloved grandchildren but God's children as well, infinite in worth and possibility.

This book is an invitation to consider grandparenting as a spiritual and ethical vocation. As

we commit ourselves to love and pray for our grandchildren, we can also work to create a just and healthy world for all grandchildren.

Paperback Price: $12.99

Kindle Price: $4.99

Anamchara
Books

www.AnamcharaBooks.com